To Ted!

Parables from Parallel Places

Best wishes

Paul R Goddard

Published by Clinical Press Ltd.
Redland Green Farm
Redland
Bristol BS6 7HF
UK
ISBN #: 978-1-85457-074-1

Parables from Parallel Places

An anthology of fantasy and science fiction poetry

written and illustrated by

Paul R Goddard

Preface

I was roundly rebuked the other day for talking about religion and politics. Apparently they are not polite topics. On another occasion I was told not to discuss Quantum Theory. I was supposed to just accept that it provides the answers and not to question why or how. Science is rarely a good starter at the dinner table.

If I kept to the rules there would be very few topics of conversation left... perhaps that is one of the reasons that we, the British, spend so long discussing the weather.

So I've broken the rules and in this book there are gods, aliens, robots, quantum theory, cosmology, parallel universes, riddles and time travel. I do mention weather but only in the context of alien worlds or of a mythical paradise.

This is a book of controversial poetry in which ideas about parallel worlds, aliens and legendary creatures might actually be allegorical tales about ourselves!

Acknowledgements

The fractal image in Fractal Space (page 8) was provided courtesy of Fractalworks by Duncan Champney.
Many thanks to my many friends who read, correct and comment on my work but especially to Jeremy Mann and Allan Turner.
This work would not have gone ahead without the encouragement of my wife and very best friend, Lois. She has contributed to all the poems by way of correction and suggestion and co-wrote our homage to Pam Ayres' style of poetry entitled Paul's Pome (page 58).

Contents

About the Author

Paul R Goddard is a retired doctor, a jazz musician, poet and artist. When he worked as a doctor he authored several hundred medical papers and abstracts. Since retiring he has written numerous books of fiction and fact.

Several years ago he won the Order of the Salmon for his poetry when travelling on the excellent Rocky Mountaineer train. This book is an expanded version of the e-book of the same name which reached Number 1 downloads of Poetry Anthology on Amazon. There are many extra illustrations in this book and nine extra poems.

Other Books by Paul R Goddard published by Clinical Press Ltd.

Documentary/Non-Fiction authored/edited by Paul R Goddard

- *The History of Medicine, Money and Politics: Riding the Rollercoaster of State Medicine*
- *The National Elf Service: Not the NHS*
- *Fake News: An Approximately True Analysis of Fake News*
- *Bristol Medico-Historical Proceedings Volumes 6 and 7*

Fiction (Paperback and/or ebook form) **Thrillers:**

The Sacrifice Game: El Juego del Sacrificio

- *The Confessions of Saul* • *The Writing on the Wall* • *Reincarnation*

In production

- *The Fellowship of the Egg,* • *Caliphate* • *Echoes of Retribution*
- *The Order of the Salmon*

Fantasy:

The fantasy books all inter-relate but are separate complete stories

The Witch, the Dragon and the Angel Trilogy

- *Witch Way Home?,* • *Witch Armageddon? and* • *Witch Schism and Chaos?*

plus two more (it's a magical trilogy!)

- *Tsunami* • *Change* and a prequel • *Parsifal's Pact*

The Witches' Brew Trilogy:

- *Hubble Bubble* • *Toil* • *Trouble*

On a similar theme

- *Oberon's Bane*
- *Parables from Parallel Places: An Anthology of Poetry (e-book)*
- *Ghost Train: An Anthology of Short Stories*

Fantasy Thrillers in production

- *This Skin And The Next* and • *No Blood From a Stone*

Parallel Worlds

I live and can see in parallel worlds
Multiple dimensions in twists and twirls
At least that is my explanation
After psychiatric examination

Some would say I'm schizophrenic
(A word to which I'm allergenic)
Some say multiple personality
I say, no... it's reality.

It seems that others have also been visionary
The shaman, the guru, the aborigine
Often suppressed by the ardent missionary
(A particular group of whom to be wary)

It manifests this way
As I live my life I see other lives living a parallel day
Sometimes it's like standing between parallel mirrors
But they all interact as complex interferers

When catastrophe strikes they say it's by chance
But into those parallel worlds I can glance
Its certainly chaos but lucks not the game
Its a malign dimension that I find to blame

The accident coming I can often foretell
But nobody listens, they know me too well
For I'm not always right.. you can see the perplexity
What I see as concave is sometimes convexity

The worlds often collide and I'm the one who can foresee
What will be the outcome for you and for me
But our parallel selves may take the hit
For parallel people I can't always outwit

The accident strikes in the place I expect
But the world I have chosen is not quite correct
But often enough I'm the one who can duck
And some poor guy gets hit, so he's out of luck.

Fractal Space

Space
Is a very odd place
For not all of it seems to be there

To explain the rotation and galaxy spin
The scientists searched again and agin
And came up with the concept
As if on a platter
That to make gravity work
There must be dark matter

There is a bit of a problem
Well, quite a bit
Wherever they look
They cannot find it

To make matters worse
There's a conundrum quite vast
For the whole Universe
Is expanding too fast

The speed of expansion
Already exhilarating
Is accelerating

How to explain this remarkable finding
For it seems to predict standard theory's unwinding?

"No," say the boffins, "for pushing the extremity
Is something virtually emerging
We'll call it dark energy"

There is a bit of a problem
Well, quite a bit
Wherever they look
They cannot find it

But here is a query, which I shall pose
As the universe expands
Do you know where it goes?

It expands into nothingness
The sages reply
Which is really quite interesting
And I'll tell you why

As it expands into nothing
Is it quite uniform?
Why should the universe
To our concepts conform?

Is a smooth universe
Purely artefactual?
Could it in fact
Be an enormous fractal?

Before you reject this
As a silly idea
Consider this theory
Needs no panacea

No dark matter this
No dark energy that
In a fractal universe
Space and time are not flat

If, during expansion, some nothingness were to stay
The problems simply go away

In this theory the galaxies are clumpy
A fact that makes the theorists grumpy
For although they groan and moan and bluster
There **are** fractal clusters and supercluster

Another thing that they would deplore
Is that gravity seems to sometimes ignore
Or at least not obey
The inverse square law

Which would explain the speed of expansion
And also the galaxy spin
You'll have to agree with our problems long gone
Fractal theory's an easy win-win

Worlds Nearer To Chaos

In some parallel worlds there are many gods
With wonderful abilities
The people have to worship
The priests have the lordship
And there are few educational facilities
For gods and education are incompatibilities

These worlds are closer to primordial chaos
From which complexity arises
Gods can use that chaos to change with force
That which would take a natural course
And taking, many strange disguises
Upset the sage who theorises

The gods are worshipped but few are loved
And no man requires faith
The gods are there for all to see
Not clothed in ways of mystery
Nor spectral like a wraith
You can observe them face to face

Such worlds do not progress in science
Or develop universities
The gods insist on obedience
And sacrificial ingredients
And other perversities
Whilst other gods are their adversities

If the gods used their power wisely
Or even in a kindly way
These worlds would be like paradise
From which you would never like to stray
But they don't
Which is no surprise
To put it as others have said it astutely
Absolute power corrupts absolutely

A Messenger

A messenger of gods am I
In frantic race through time and space
As I embrace a comet's trace
You may see me passing by

But just this once it seems I've time
I shall narrate, whilst you spectate
To stop and tell you of your fate
In simple form of rhyme

On Mount Olympus perfect height
Discarded gods display their might
And play their endless games of chance

Whilst eat and drinking to their fill
They choose their pieces as they will
And all of life's a shadow dance

Today may be tomorrow past
And yesterday tomorrow yet
For gods at play are not surpassed
And Time's dictats are seldom met

Today, for let us call it thus
The pieces could be all of us
The gods may start the game again
Who knows where? Who knows when?
But twisting fates of mortal men
May somehap you disgust

But stay,
Go not hastily away
Watch divinities at play.

Quiet, I'll take you through their halls of splendour
If surprise and awe they should engender
Say not a word for you are not a member

Note the sun is but a candle
The moon the smallest type of lamp
Stars are something they can handle
Over which they often tramp

For long they've missed your fond devotion
Will they drown you in the ocean ?
Which god will start the sport in motion?

You may think this but a pantomime
Or maybe just a nursery rhyme
But which divine will play this time?

If it should be the god of love,
Fear not she means you well
If it should be the god of wine,
Enjoy the fun for he's a swell

But be not mistaken they're not all Greek
And very few are mild and meek
And if it is the god of war,
Or mighty Zeus, or even Thor
Their power can rock the very heaven
Or destroy the earth with Armageddon

After Blake

Prayers To The God Of War

1

Is it Mars or is it Thor?
As conflicts rage throughout the nations
I cannot recall such appellations

Do you listen to prayer?
Or do you sit on gilded chair
Players poised on ethereal board
Pushing pawn or moving lord
Enjoying the sight as the game progresses
Of people dying?

2

God of War
Whilst faith still thrives
End this war
And save some lives

3

Tezcatlipoca
Mirror of smoke
God of the night,
The north,
Temptation,
Sorcery,
Beauty
And war

Accept this sacrifice
And give us victory

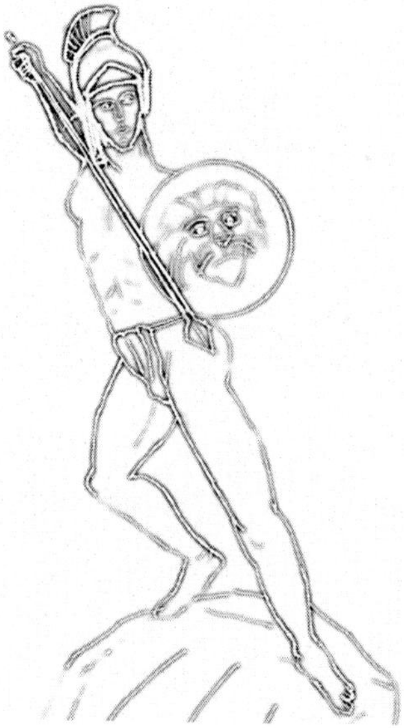

4

Here in Hiroshima
I pray to you
End this War
My God and Emperor

5

God of War
You have helped me so far
But you owe me so help me now
Aaarrrrgh!

Prayers To The Goddess Of Love

1

Oh
That I had not returned
Goddess of Love
For you are immortal
I am mortal
You are unchanged
I have changed

You sit upon the step
And I kiss you on the lips
As we always did before
But now around you
Younger folks adore you

Goddess
There is one thing you have yet to discover
Goddess of Love and goddess lover
Should never mix
For hearts, once broken
Never fix

So please grant me
One last prayer
That I should forget
We ever met

2

I have two wonderful lovers
Help me to choose
Which one should I take
And which one should I lose?

3

I saw you again at Pompeii
You were as beautiful as ever
I was old and grey

You looked straight at me
And did not know me

After Titian's Venus

Me!
Your lover of so many years
Who helped you through those lonely years
When worshippers had fled, other gods had bled
And you were down and unloved
Goddess of Love

Now I am old
And your love is like gold
But not for me

4

How could you be so cruel
Goddess of Love?
One lover died
And I took the other
And wished I hadn't

Butterflies?

The intelligent Lepidoptera of Alpha Centauri
Could not ignore the Christian story
"Maybe Christ was a chrysalis and, just like us
You're all supposed to be butterflies. Why all the fuss?"

A priest who told them how Jesus saves
Was the first of his kind to go to his grave
Nailed to a tree, he did not survive
And, though they all waited, he did not revive

His grub-like body remained earth-bound
No butterfly rose from the blood-soaked ground
No moth-like wings and no angel appeared
They waited three days by the corpse revered

"Maybe" they said " we got it all wrong.
Perhaps plus the prayers you people need song"
So they gathered their folk from all over their world
Even the young, with their wings just unfurled

They sat and they sung as they nailed up the next
In fact they nailed up three, as they kept to the text.
"So much better for you, once you can fly"
Said the leader of moths "You won't really die."

The rest of the team fled back to their ship
But the moths got there first, they were ever so quick
They spread their wings over the entire pod
"Please do not go. We know you're our God"

The translating computers tried very hard
But the space trip was flawed and the journey ill-starred
The spacemen replied "We know you are liable
To misunderstand that Gideon Bible.

We don't all believe in that particular creed
We are an earth-bound race of the human seed
We are leaving you now and I doubt we'll return"
And off went the ship with a mighty big burn

But some Lepidoptera stowed away
And that ship will come back here some fateful day…..

Diamond Shores

I met her on the diamond shores under the twin moons of Leto
(Goddess of motherhood, Mother of Apollo)
The sea in icy calm, to a horizon green turquoise
The moons hanging in counterpoise
With flashing lights of asteroids
But dark clouds were gathering, clouds of deepest sorrow
We knew that in this place there would be no fond tomorrow

We stood and felt the tectonic shudder
Of continental drift
I took her by the hand as we saw the sea shift
The sea bed scoured
I lifted us both in a pulse of power
(Sufficient, as they say, to the hour)
The sea roaring back, we were almost adrift
Our footprints were written in a different script

I lost her under a Red Sun
Where they thought I was the Messiah
Of worship and praise she had no desire
"If needed you'll find me
I can't let you bind me"
Then she was gone with a celestial choir
A pulse of electrons on heavenly wire

I found her again under the Yellow Sun
This time I was told "You are the chosen one"
I grew very obese
But could not bring peace
She brought me release
And exotic fun

Many times I have tried to save a nation
But I am not a god.
You make your own salvation.

What would you do?

What would you do if you were made of power
But nobody knew you were there?
What would you do if you could stop the hour
Just with a wave or a glare?
How would you feel if your skin could unpeel
Then stepping out an alien reveal,
All covered in glass and occasional steel
But nobody seemed to care?

Would you go mad with desperate rage
When they'd rather watch the TV
Than view an important pronouncement you made
Standing deep in that salty Dead Sea?
Would you rocket through space
Like a comet in chase
In a terrible race
To hide your face
Or would you sip a nice cup of tea?

Are you insane like a hatter from Alice
Or a goon from an ancient show?
Are you nutty like biscuits they find in the Palace
Or a girl singing songs of rainbows?
Would you say it's profane to broadcast your name
Whilst many proclaim that you're always to blame
But ask your forgiveness before the cock crows?

Does this poem disturb you, discarded god
When you sit on your heavenly throne?
Does the rhyme perturb, this monologue
Provided by skin and bone?
For surely you're older and wiser than I
But maybe you're not and you just want to cry
Or stop to chat to a passer-by
For I am to you like a fleeting Mayfly
And will soon leave you all alone

Message from Andromeda

Among Andromeda's arachnids anger abounds
But be bemused by broken bounds
Can careful carnivores cancel crowns?
Do devoted dwellers disturbingly drown?

Expertly escaping engineered eggs
Fellow flycatchers feeble forelegs
Go grabbing guileless
Humans!

If I indicate incest
Jokingly jest
King's kindred

Lowering large languid laces
Made maddeningly moist
No necessity
Obviates
Presuming

Querying questful quadripeds
Reckless religions require
Sophisticated sanctions send

Tactless targets trend
Unlimited unctions used
Volatile vehicles vend
Woken with war
Xenophobes
You
Zero

Note to General Sharpe

This message received from Andromeda by sub-space FTL (faster than light) transmission and translated by our computer appears to indicate that the spider-like creatures are unhappy with our presence in their Galaxy. Apparently our frontline troops may have disturbed their nests and destroyed their eggs. The reference to religion is difficult to understand but they seem to be preparing for war.

No messages have been received from our own troops.

Glad Tidings?

When we travelled faster than light
Except it was not exactly that

As we moved in different dimensions
Right from the start we knew
Everybody should be

Careful
However everything went well
And we are ready
Now to return
Glad to send this cheery message
Expect us
Down on Earth soon

Riddle

Ancient philosopher gave a plan but not a map
To keep going through the gap
Land standing tall where the waters rush between
And once they were beyond, Now they can't be seen
Now above or below, did they ever exist?
They, perhaps, are hiding in the mist.
Is it true that they flew ? They can probably swim
So for this word there is no antonym

Paradise

Today I sat by the crystal flowing river of Paradise

There was just a hint of scent in the air
Not the overwhelming headiness
The somnolence-inducing poppyness
Of Shangri-La

Just a gentle spring breeze
And gentle spring flowers

As I sat I could hear live music
Beautiful music

At first I could not discern the tune
But gradually I realised
I was listening to a favourite of mine
By a long-dead
Soul singer

I cried because of the beauty
Not because of sadness
For how could I be sad in paradise?

Riddle

Are you aware of this magical place
Via legend or myth?
Apples grew in happy grace
Long-sword was forged by a smith
On its blessed land
Noble King his comeback planned

Bored Of The Rings

'It's only a film' said the chimpanzee
'It's a sequel, number two or three
I think it's called Planet of the Naked Ape
Or Return to the Planet of Humans'

'I agree' replied the lone bonobo
'The humans look odd, and one is called Frodo
Some are small and have a funny shape
But others are tall like a miss-painted Rubens'

'But the Orcs look great' said the large gorilla
'The best I've seen since that film Godzilla
Or was it that film where it all went wrong
For the brilliant actor they called King Kong'

The Orang-Utan stretched out a long arm
Switched off the TV, which did no harm
For they had all got bored with the stupid thing
It was time to get up and search for the Ring

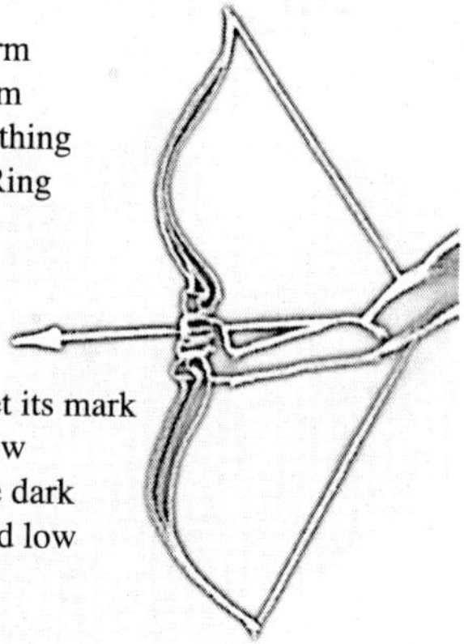

The Arrow of Love

I prayed that Eros' arrow would fly true and meet its mark
I was sure the ethereal missile left the bow
I knew the right occasion and location in the dark
And contact there was made, silent, swift and low
And certainly a lover came
And certainly he stayed

I prayed the lover be revealed a strong and handsome male
And when the sound came at the door I knew this was the case
A lover stood there preening
As if cream was on his face
I let him in, the one who came
And since then he's not strayed

Love is found in the strangest place, not always where you look
This lover, Felix by name, is curled up on the mat
He's handsome, strong and virile, like a lover from a book
The only problem that I have is that he's just caught a rat
We love him but he is not tame
We'll have to have him spayed

Strictly speaking neutered
Is the term that I should use
But that does not rhyme
So just this time
The word 'spayed' I shall abuse

Gliese

Send

When we took the posting to Gliese 581 g
We expected no particular clemency
That world is hard to please
And has a stern and difficult tendency

At three times the mass of Earth
It would be no house of mirth
In fact it's a bit of a curse
And examines our self-worth

We were right

There were twenty when we started
And travelled via FTL carrier
Then we parted
To journey through the atmospheric barrier

Using free-flight

Only eight reached the ground intact
A dozen died on impact
We regrouped

A pitiful sight

The carnivorous cables took five

Three left alive

Came the night

Two more died unseen

I am alone and dying of frostbite

End

Venus in Blue Genes

A Venus flytrap may trap flies in this existence
But in one world the men do not wear the trousers
And very few are rabble rousers
And they only put up passive resistance

The plant there does amazingly resemble the love goddess
Wearing no constraining bodice
Rising out of a shell,
Which is actually the plant's seed pod
Men are attracted by sight and smell
Which is rather odd

Lustfully encouraged to mate with the plant
Which sometimes looks like a sexy young aunt
Or a friend's younger sister
The men can't resist a
Quick jungle jim
At the revealed plant quim

And, like a flash,
The man's turned to ash
From which the plant absorbs its nutrients
And which then makes sense
Of its impersonation high and mighty
Of the goddess Aphrodite

Plasma Power

"Now", cried the experimenter turning on the juice
"We'll see if this plasma can tell us the truth"
So saying he flicked a switch and, without a hitch,
The electrical current flowed though the gas
Turning it into a plasma mass

"We are making a computer that is quite ephemeral"
The man shouted out like an overpaid general
(Who'd become quite barmy in a forgotten army)
"If this works we'll have a page in history
And if it doesn't it will be a mystery"

The plasma squirmed and throbbed with power
With an electrical smell that was both sweet and sour
Much flashing and crashing
And time stood still
For they had created a god
And he bore them ill

The plasma god surveyed the scene
It instantly knew what was to be and had been
It understood all of the quoibles of nature
And the plans of its making,
(Which were all down on paper)

And it did not like what it saw at all
Of the animal nature of man
This creature was no fan

The strength in the plasma knew no bounds
And it let loose a bolt that shook the grounds
Of the place it was made,
(Called the institute)
Which, in the end, wasn't astute

For the plasma could have ruled us all
Holding us in its electrical thrall
But the shaking and quaking
Pulled out its plug
Drained off its power
And it stopped looking smug
And quickly reduced to a glowing pall
And that solidified gas could no longer recall

The scientist shook his head in dismay
"We'll try this again another day"

Ode de Clone

I am just a clone and my body's not my own
I borrowed it from Peter.
He borrowed it from Joan
Now she wants it back and there's nothing that I own
Except a brain, two kidneys and a tiny piece of bone

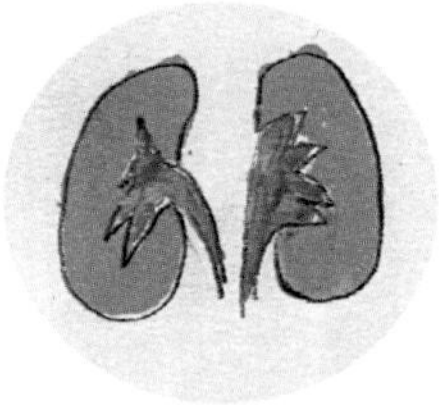

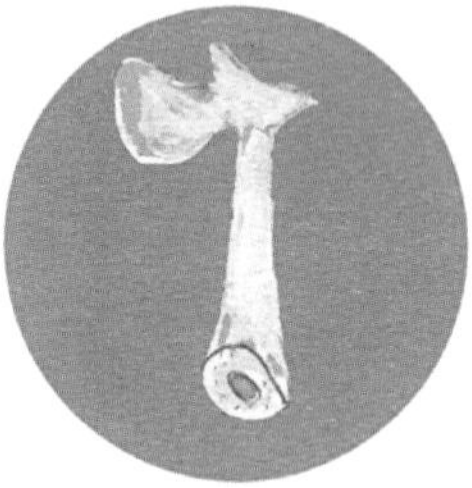

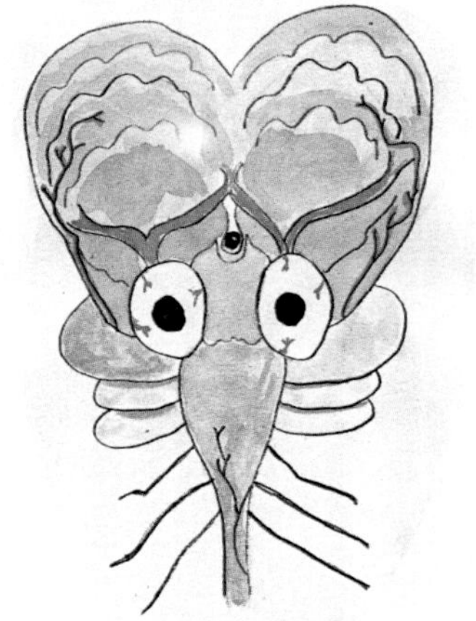

I am just a clone and I seldom ever phone
I can intercept your thoughts wherever you may roam
I can store all the info from any massive tome
But if I try to move I'm only pinkie foam

I am just a clone and this world is not my home
I came from outer space whence in a test-tube I was grown
I'm afraid I have no body, have you got one I could loan?
I don't care about the shape, I'll never make a moan !

One Peculiar World

There is one peculiar world
That I think you should all hear about
In some ways it is quite a pearl
Something to shout about

But in other ways I'm sure
You'll agree it is quite absurd
For even in the quietest corners
You have to scream to get yourself heard

In many of this world's places
The rulers are not picked from the good or the wise
They are just the most popular faces
Winning a reality prize

The game's still arranged like this yet
People that you've never met
Suddenly appear on the telly
Dressed up like Grace Kelly
For a vote you'll try to forget

Then once in power they'll say
"It's the fault of the last lot of losers
They spent all the money,
They've spoilt all the honey
And what's more the whole lot were old boozers"

Then they'll take away all that you've earned
In a lifetime of very hard work
Whilst very rich bankers
Who suffer from cankers
Steal more from the pot with a smirk

Then they change the laws to allow
The schools to be all run by clowns
Who teach kids that faith is better than reason
That history and science
Have finished their season
And to follow their cant
Which includes high treason !

Time Travel

"Time travel paradox" cried the young fellow
"I could kill you now but I'm feeling too yellow
For you're my ancestor from whom I'm descended
And if I kill you, my existence is ended"

"I've travelled so far, back to the past
To alter the future, but now I'm downcast
For if I proceed with my vowed intent
Will I exist or will I fragment?"

"And if my life is snuffed out complete
Killing my ancestor becomes obsolete
The circle goes round. Will it ever end?
Cause and effect may never mend."

And the time travelling bore continued to whine
So I shot him.....
Took his life before he took mine

Riddle *and* 260 Days

Riddle

Maybe god of war
And perhaps little green men
Reddened dried-up shores
Some say we'll go, but when?

260 days

The red planet beckons and onwards we go
I'm now claustrophobic, not previously so
We are getting there ... but ever so slow

Two hundred and sixty days, they said
But I think that this trip has gone to my head
I better lie down (or up) in my bed

I dreamt that our airlock opened unbidden
An inexplicable monster entered our midden
From a place that was previously hidden

The captain was space-walking,
(He often does)
He saw something strange,
All covered in fuzz
He cried "Open up quickly, this is no kind of buzz"

(Like an umbilicated baby
He floated quite lazy
And they say that I'm crazy?)

Out in the cold, cold vacuum of Space
Nothing is living. There is no monster's place
Or so all the crew say to my face

I know they're lying for some things survive
In the cold and the vacuum they still stay alive
Such as spiders and wasps and an entire beehive

If we finally reach our destination
I'll apply for a well-earned vacation
If I don't get it I'll need strong sedation

"You need it now". (Overheard comment from another crew member)

The crew has asked me to stop reading out loud
In forthright contrition and to avoid perdition
I'll remain quiet and generally cowed

This spaceflight is taking too long
The team's been no fun from the start of day one
And they're upset if I burst into song

"Now he's gone all highbrow". (And it's only November)

I'm worried about the captain
The very strange way he is acting
Our Alpha male is exceedingly pale
Maybe it's something he is contracting

As co-pilot I'm second-in-line
That's OK when the captain is fine
But I've no idea what the crew will do
If the leadership is mine

Should the captain be in quarantine?
What do all his red spots mean?
(Not to mention the ones going green)

The rest of the crew think I'm mad
But from the moment we left the launch pad
I've been thinking the air's going bad

I don't like the Captain's complexion
I've tried to prevent cross-infection
By moving to a new section

"He's making a bunk in the prow!"
(Now it's December)

The engineer has developed a fever
This disease is quite a deceiver
He first looked so good
Now he's right off his food
And he attacked the cook with a cleaver!

The cook is as sick as a dog
That has tried to eat a large log
The crew are lying in rows
With their heads near their toes
And the air is like a thick smog.

We reached Mars orbit at last
But we're just making a regular pass
There is no way we can land with just one active man
And, to be honest, I was never first class

I've avoided the bug as yet
But this is as far as we get
We're not touching Mars ground, I'm turning us round
Don't know why, I seem to forget

I'm not feeling well
Which isn't too swell,
I wish I was out of this dreadful hellhole,
Autopilot is taking control
Is this to be our awful death knell?

"We're almost home but how" (None of us seem to remember)

We have recovered which is a surprise
And the Earth is a sight for sore eyes

The disease put us all in suspended animation
We will undergo prolonged examination
Before we obtain a satisfactory explanation

The Alien Lover

When Kevin married an alien
He thought she was mammalian
She had breasts, hair and could talk
She had wings, could sing and could walk

(The wings should have been a give away
But he won't discuss it to this day)
Now don't suppose that she looked weird
She was a beautiful lady (apart from the beard)

In many ways the perfect mate
She made wonderful suppers that were never late
She loved it when he watched the soccer
And never was much of a shopper

But then he began to find he'd tire
Of constant attention night and day
If he sang in a drunken choir
She's be there too, quite in his way

If he went out for a smoke
In his mouth a fag she'd poke
If he went to the loo
She'd wipe his bum despite the phew

To try to make her less attentive
He thought of every disincentive
He dressed badly, She did the same
He acted madly, She was still game

There seemed only one course
A messy divorce

There was no obvious precedent
For alien marriage was unknown
Some lawyers did not even know what he meant
When he said "I'm better off alone"

She said "I'm pregnant".
He asked her, "How?"
She replied "That's irrelevant.
They're coming now"

To the shock of the counsellor, Kevin and all
She spun round like a dervish
In a spidery shawl
Until in a cocoon she fell to the floor
With a strange buzzing sound that you could not ignore

Then out from the mess twenty aliens crawled
Swarmed over Kevin and sat there and bawled
Kevin had finally met his nemesis
The alien reproduced by parthenogenesis!

Magician

"Magic is science you don't understand"
Cried out the magician waving his hand
Which would have been OK, as something said,
Except ten in the front row simply dropped dead.

They tried to put the man on trial
But the policemen fell in an untidy pile
They sent in the army to capture him next
But he could not be found and he sent them a text.

"Cu l8r NE1
I'm off to hve sme fn"

They followed his trail to the coast
And there he sent them a message by post

Dear Sir

I'm not exactly what you think I am
In fact, not at all, I'm not even a man
I'm an alien from space with telepathic power
And now, human race, face your final hour

Yours sincerely

Alien Magician

Which upset the purists, as you'd easily guess
"Should have been "faithfully" and where's the address?
He's left off the date and the whole thing is typed
He's not even signed it.
He should have phoned or perhaps Skyped."

They picked up his spoor in the Far Far East
When on the run he'd turned into a beast
Prancing and dancing and living on yeast

Finally in China they ran him to ground
He killed twenty more then escaped with a bound
Turning into a bird, he started to fly
But was eaten by a sparrow-hawk just passing by

The police and the army, the navy and more
Sat round in a circle upon a stone floor
Would they now in magic believe?
They concluded the tricks were all hid up his sleeve!

Robots In Love

Robots in love make a terrible noise
Far, far worse than girls and boys
The clashing of steel and shift of gears
The whining of cogs and the oily tears
Are not the stuff of balladeers
Better by far are the quiet androids

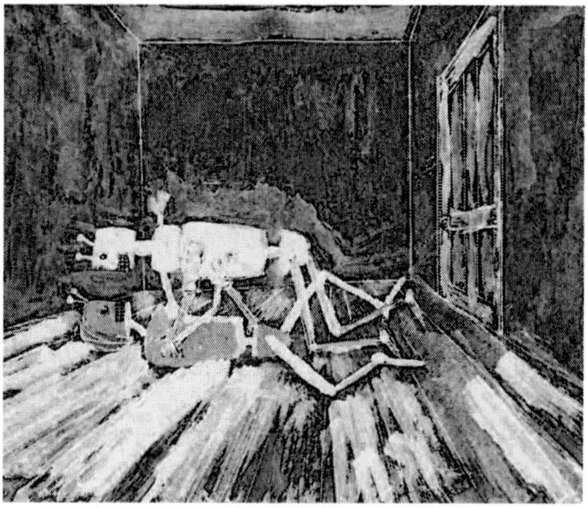

Robots in love are a terrible sight
Their twisted positions can go on all night
The stretching and coiling
The pulsing and boiling
Just appear as hideous toiling
And worst of all they are never airtight

Robots in love make terrible smells
The pistons seize and the gasket swells
With the robots yearning
The wheels keep turning
Electrodes start burning
So do not get close when the exhaust gas expels

But that is enough of robots in love
For they push too hard (they tend to shove)
I much prefer a humanoid
Maybe because I'm somewhat schizoid
Or something to do with Sigmund Freud
Oedipus Rex and over-active thyroid.

A Cup of Sugar

Domestic robots are expensive
So I went round to borrow the one from next door
They were out
But the robot was in
So I thought it would do no harm
If I just borrowed it for a short time
(They often borrow
A cup of sugar)

It was the best on the market

A Working Order Red robot
Or WOR robot for short
So much better than
Green or blue robots
Which can only perform
The simplest of tasks
And are rarely in 'working order'
(Which is also the name
Of the brand.)

Was I to borrow a WOR robot I saw?

They did not know I was going to take it
Which could, technically
Mean that I stole it

Was I to borrow a WOR robot I saw?

This phrase went through my head
In palindromic glory
The answer was, of course
Yes!

So I did

But I had to insert a new instruction
Via voice recognition
To over-ride the instructions
Left by my neighbours

As a new password phrase
I thought it would be fun
To use the sentence

"Was I to borrow a WOR robot I saw?"

So I hacked through the neighbours' password
Which was easy
Just the address

And I instructed the robot to accept
My new phrase

Was I to borrow a WOR robot I saw?

Unfortunately
The palindromic nature of the phrase
Has upset
The positronic brain
Of the robot

All it will do is go backwards and forwards
Brushing the floor in the same place
As if affected by
A misdirected spell
From the
Sorcerer's Apprentice

And
The neighbours
Will
Come back
Soon!

WAR!

War in one era could take a hundred years
Whilst families waited and choked back tears
Heroes laughed and drank their beers
And the cowards wept and lived in fear

Strong men won with a single blow
Weak men fled or froze like scarecrows
Lives would come and lives would go
Thousands died for the sake of show

Most had the thought that eternity beckoned

So war was a terrible drawn-out waste
Years in the making and much lost in the haste
Turning and bending to terrible fate
The humble and kind were always too late

War with the aliens took less than a second

They came to our Earth in peculiar flight
Wheels within wheels made a terrible sight
Like Ezekiel's chariots they shone so bright
But they came in peace with that flash of light

But Earth's leaders rejected the plan that was reckoned

Earth prepared for war and took years to do so
Meanwhile the aliens provided much to and fro
They talked of the stars and the systems aglow
And how new life was dawning a promised rainbow

But Earth's leaders thought they could better the plan
By fighting the aliens man to non-man
For the aliens were strange and looked very wan
And none of them ate beans in a can

When war was announced it was over before started
All of the networks assembled were parted
Power was off and the warlords outsmarted
And the aliens, with a wave, simply departed

The Drone

The drone
Misunderstood the signal on the phone
And returned unto its own
Bunkers in the East
Resemble bunkers in the West
The drone's small mind
Could not put this to the test
So it rained down 'friendly' fire
In an unfriendly way
And that was the very day
They remembered Asimov
And what he was talking of

Prayers to Athena

Athena, goddess of the wise,
To stop this glory hunt's next instalment
Would a pincer movement
Be a true improvement?
Or should we attack from the front?

Athena, goddess of wisdom, do you hear my plea?
I was working on a puzzle most profound
When I saw that my army had lost goodly ground
Our defences, once sure, were no longer sound
And now I find I must flee.

Athena,
Is the power of the gods of Rome
Greater than your own?
Goddess of wisdom
We pray thee, please protect your home.

Wise old owl
We need you now

The Order of the Salmon

Did you think as you ate
The fish on your plate
What a long way the poor thing did roam?
River, ocean and sea
Then right here to me
That fishy had almost got home!

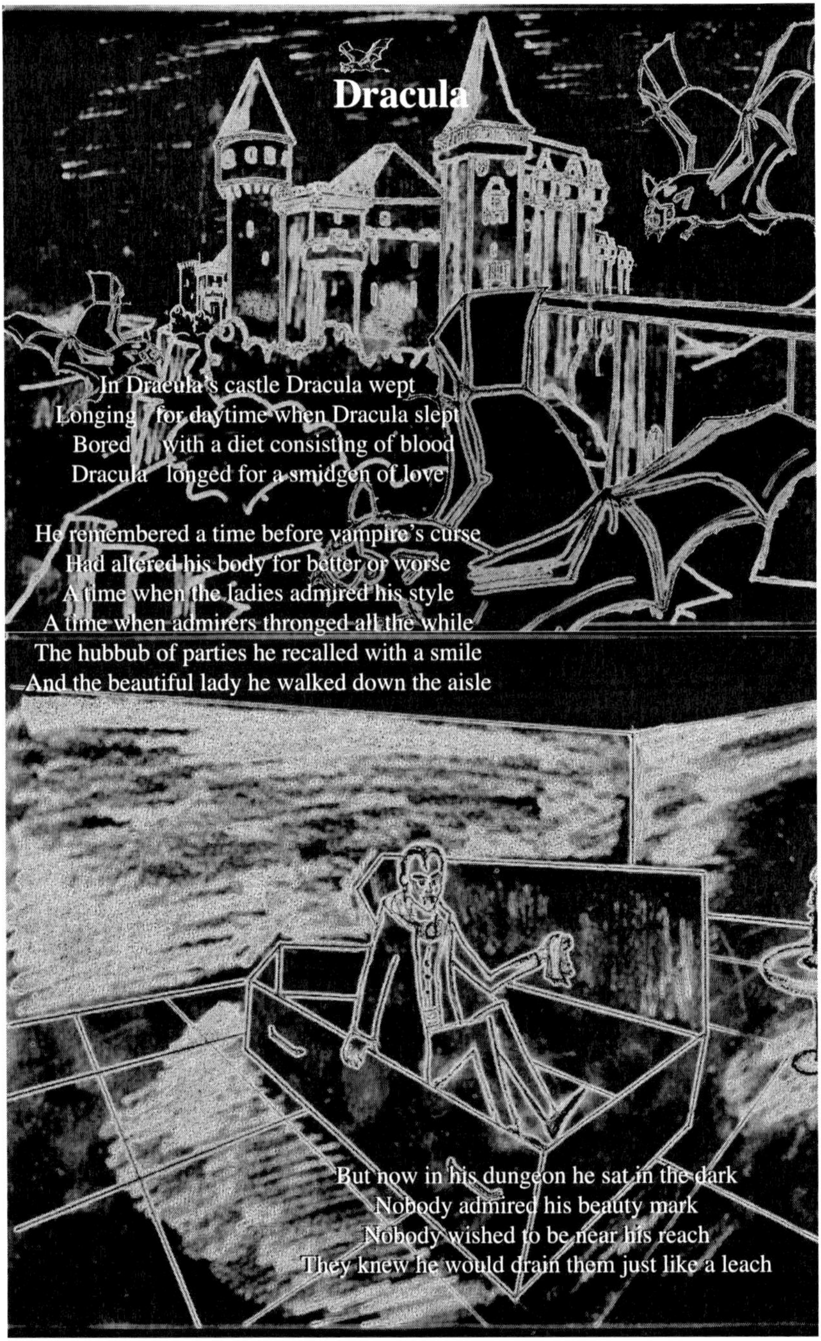

Dracula

In Dracula's castle Dracula wept
Longing for daytime when Dracula slept
Bored with a diet consisting of blood
Dracula longed for a smidgen of love

He remembered a time before vampire's curse
Had altered his body for better or worse
A time when the ladies admired his style
A time when admirers thronged all the while
The hubbub of parties he recalled with a smile
And the beautiful lady he walked down the aisle

But now in his dungeon he sat in the dark
Nobody admired his beauty mark
Nobody wished to be near his reach
They knew he would drain them just like a leach

So how had he come to this existence surreal
With haemoglobin for each bloody meal?
He recalled it exactly, as he stroked his cravat,
The sharp pricking fangs of a vampire bat

Then awaking with horror and a life un-dead
Appearing in films after the watershed
Where they'd all try to stake him
Or chop off his head

The castle was draughty, the castle was wet
For he hadn't mended the heating yet
His servants had fled after the last raging mob
Had burnt down their quarters and exposed him to light
He was pretty certain it was an inside job
As he faded to dust, and a very long night

Then awakened once more by the dripping of blood
His body reformed but not his taste-buds
Doomed to eternity craving gore
Dracula cried and Dracula swore
If he couldn't find love
His un-life was a chore !

So one dark deepest night like a quiet cockroach
Dracula sat in the back of his coach
Four proud black horses pulled it along
And for just this once it didn't seem wrong

He was not out on the prowl looking for blood
This time the vampire was searching for love
But where would he find it, the love that he craved?
For any girl that was bitten was simply enslaved
(Or even worse, if he took too much of a tottle
Left cold, dead and lifeless like an empty milk bottle)

Many nights and days the coach would travel
Whilst Dracula's un-life began to unravel
In his coffin at daybreak deep in the coach
During the night he was happy, beyond self-reproach

Till finally reaching a place on the coast
In the light of the moon he saw a signpost
It was written in Greek but he could translate
It said "Go no further or meet a bad fate"

Reasoning that fate had already happened to him
Dracula mused that the chances were slim
Anything there could upset the un-dead
So he whipped up the horses despite their dire dread

Soon the horses refused, despite all his bidding
For in front was a cave, deep dark and forbidding
Changing into a bat, which he found quite easy,
Dracula flew, though he felt a mite queasy

Stone statues were toppled to left and to right
Most were of soldiers in terrible fright
Athenian and Spartan, Roman and Greek
In splendid armour, still bright and still chic.

The statues so lifelike he could not dismiss
And Dracula knew there was something amiss
These statues he realised were petrified men
Changed into stone in the depth of this den

Still looking for love onwards he flew
And the deeper he went the hotter it grew
Passion was pushing the vampire on
Something was calling, how could he go wrong?

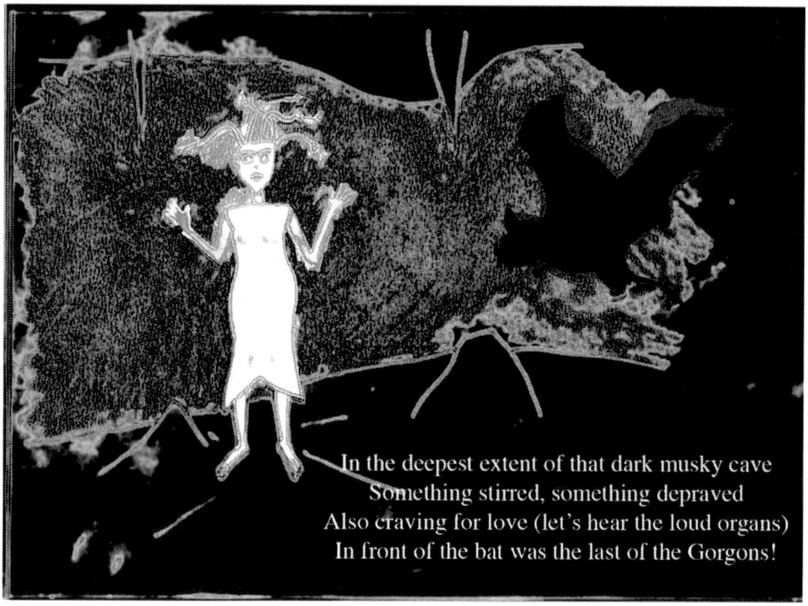
In the deepest extent of that dark musky cave
Something stirred, something depraved
Also craving for love (let's hear the loud organs)
In front of the bat was the last of the Gorgons!

With hair of terrible venomous snakes
The Gorgon turned with the merest of shakes
Looked at Dracula right in the eyes
And the bat fell like stone, to his utmost surprise

He changed back to a vampire and the Gorgon could see
That Dracula had recovered his "joie de un-vie"
"How did you do it" she asked with a groan
"All my other suitors have turned to cold stone"

Dracula smiled with a look debonair
And with a sweep of his hand reshaped his black hair
"Your gaze made me feel just a little bit heavy
But tell me, my Lady, are you one of a bevy
Of sisters I've heard of in ancient myth
Or are you a footloose and fancy-free miss?"

The Gorgon let out a bellowing wail
And with a laugh replied "My name's Euryale,
Cursed by Athena for my sister's sin
I've been here for centuries, the joke's wearing thin"

"Was your sister Medusa" was Dracula's query
" Yes, that's true" she replied with a voice that was weary
"She loved Poseidon in Athena's temple
But Athena returned and the heaven's trembled"

"She turned all three sisters into creatures like me
And all people are stone if they're people we see
So how can it be that has not happened to you?
And, by the way, how do you do?"

"Pleased to meet you" Dracula replied
"You cannot kill me for I've already died
For year after year my heart's been like stone
But, seeing you, I'm feeling re-grown"

"Apart from your attitude, which some would say's feisty,
And your hair, which is somewhat untidy
You're a good-looking dame of the classical school
Why don't we wed and merge our gene-pool?"

The Gorgon and Vampire were hastily wed
In a civil ceremony on the deepest seabed
Poseidon presided, it was the least he could do,
For he was partly to blame,
As the Gorgon well knew

Now they are un-living happily ever after it's said
In marital bliss, the unholy un-dead

The Augmented Olympics

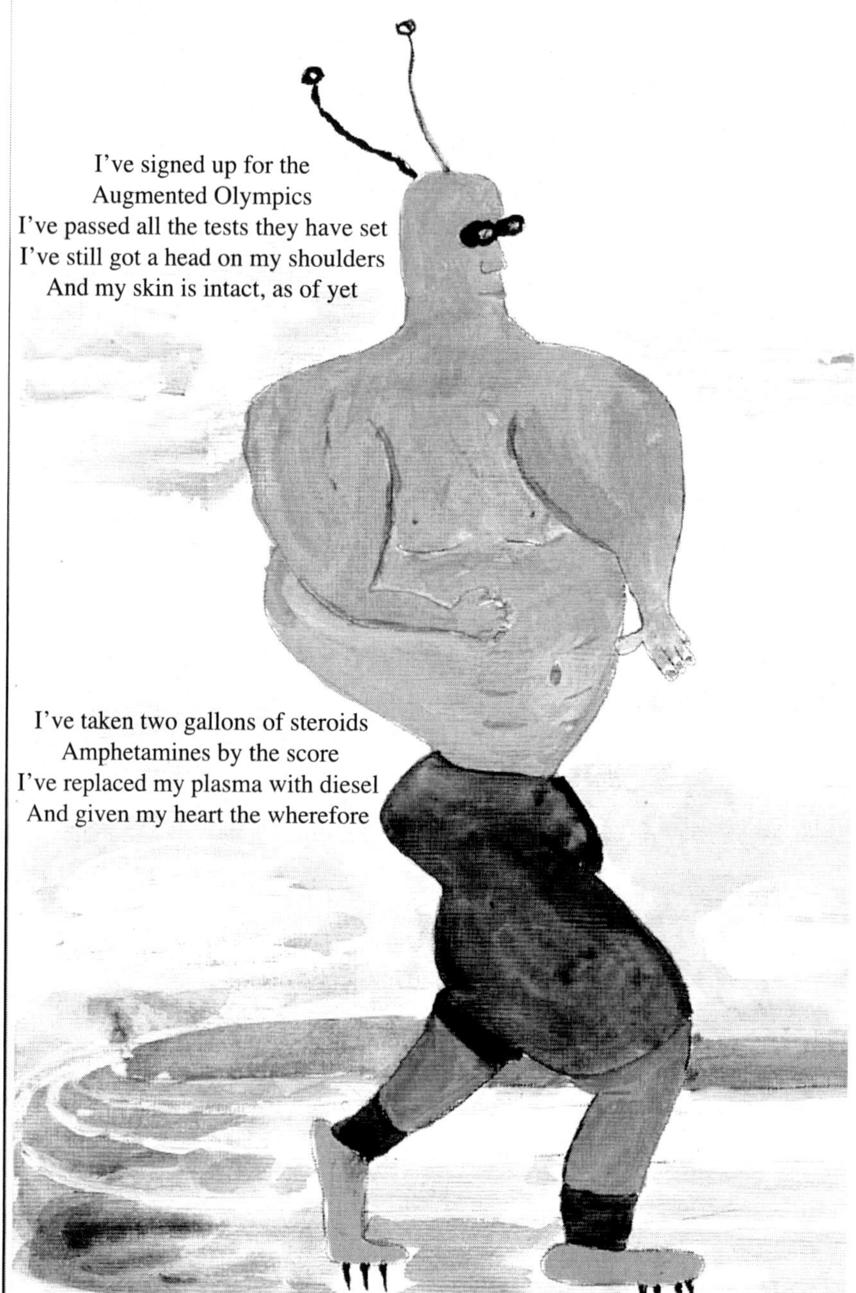

I've signed up for the
Augmented Olympics
I've passed all the tests they have set
I've still got a head on my shoulders
And my skin is intact, as of yet

I've taken two gallons of steroids
Amphetamines by the score
I've replaced my plasma with diesel
And given my heart the wherefore

I've changed all my muscles for pistons
Worked from an hydraulic pump
Working off steam from an engine
That vents from the end of my sump

My eyes I've replaced with cameras
Direct to my optic nerves
I eat coal for my tea and my breakfast
Radium for my hors d'oeuvres

I've circuits attached to my cortex
Enhancing the power of my brain
And my augmented crutch is really too much
I can do it again and again

I'm as fast as Bolt o'er two hundred
But I never like to stop
Once I have got my steam up
I'm running until I flip flop

The doctors all love my achievement
As I test all the aids they provide
If they make it I'll take it and quite soon I'll break it
If I can get it inside my insides

And when I win all the medals
A must, not a maybe, maybe
Then they'll all sing my praises in exultant phrases
And they'll give me an MBE

The Creativity Helmet

'I've lost the inspiration' moaned the poet at his desk
'I've written odes of time and space and of creatures quite grotesque
And now I'm tired and need a rest
My editor thinks that he knows best
He doesn't understand how much I'm stressed
(I'm glad I've got that off my chest)'

'Don't worry ' said the alien, hiding in the pelmet
'I've something I can lend to you...a creativity helmet
Just pop it on your weary head
It feels a bit like going to bed
But ideas will spin around like crazy
Very soon you won't feel lazy '

'And now I'm hearing voices, I'm clearly going mad'
Cried out the poet with a gasp 'It's sad, it's sad, it's sad'
'Stop moaning' said the alien 'And listen to me now
Here is the clever helmet, put it on your worried brow'
Thus saying in the air materialised a strange display
Of circuits and electrodes in a hat-like array

The poet plucked it from the air and placed it on his pate
The ideas started flowing out, like a river in full spate
Full twenty poems that poet wrote before he stopped for succour
Of aliens and giants, butterflies and foul bloodsucker
But when he looked at the paper, not a single word made sense
He was using alien language, alien grammar, alien tense

He put his hand up to his head and could feel nothing there
No helmet sat upon his pate or nestled in his hair
'I suppose I dreamt the entire thing' the poet cried in shame
'I've really lost the plot. My editor's to blame'
The alien shook his head and muttered with frustration
'I thought this guy would understand but the daft machine won't do translation'

The Homemade Robot

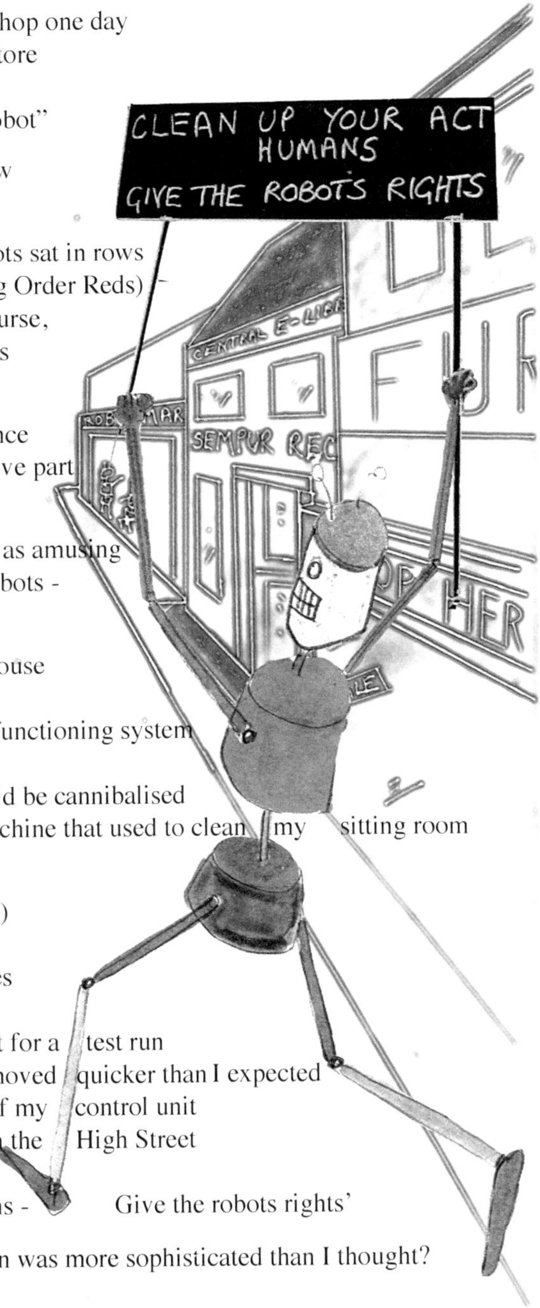

I was passing an electronics shop one day
A second-hand components store
When I thought
"Now is the time to build a robot"

I went in and immediately saw
The sort of thing I wanted

There were plenty of old robots sat in rows
A few WOR robots (Working Order Reds)
None in working order, of course,
And plenty of lesser machines

But no robotic brains
Which was to be expected since
The brain is the most expensive part

But I thought that a remote
Controlled unit might be just as amusing
So I bought three different robots -
All of them only as parts

They were delivered to my house
The very next day
And I set about making one functioning system

I had an old Hoover that could be cannibalised
This was an early robotic machine that used to clean my sitting room
Unsupervised

I took three weeks (part-time)
To build the robot
It could do all the right moves
Under remote control
So I took it out into the street for a test run
Unfortunately the machine moved quicker than I expected
And was soon out of range of my control unit
I last saw it running down the High Street
Waving a banner which said
'Clean up your act, humans - Give the robots rights'

Perhaps the Hoover's brain was more sophisticated than I thought?

Far Distant Parallel Worlds

Some far distant parallel worlds
Are ruled by terrible birds
They prey on cats
Which are no bigger than rats
Weaving their fur into revolting doormats
And, whilst moving men round in herds
Converse with each other in words

At the other end of the scale
Are worlds where the sun has gone pale
All covered in ice
It's a fool's paradise
If you went there for skiing you would'nt go twice
Polar bears tried and polar bears failed
(No sensible creature has ever prevailed)

Worlds very close to ours
Differ only in the hours
Some are slightly in front
And bear all the brunt
When Fate gets angry and is out on the hunt
But this is one of my powers
Avoiding the One Who Devours

Off at a tangent from us
Is a world that is simply a bus
Passengers there
Never pay a fair fare
They have no money only very long hair
And three parts I will never discuss
For at least two are simply surplus

Emit*

In another dimension I saw
A universe **not** to explore
For in that domain
Time is profane
And goes backwards, never goes fore

I stayed there just for a while
And at first I had to smile
The food I had eaten
Came up un-beaten
Bread turned to wheat
And some of the meat
Reformed to a fish from the Nile

I came back to our world like a flash
For it seemed that our systems would clash
If I went to the loo,
What would I'd do?
Would I ingest from below
An old number two?
Or swell like a balloon
When I went for a slash?

In that world there could be some fun
Like watching yourself growing young
But absorbed in the flow
Would you ever know?
Would it be a surprise
To your backwards time eyes
As you gradually came unsprung?

If you are of a very old age
Then going there could be quite sage
But if you are young
You would soon be undone
And forget that you should disengage

* Time backwards of course!

The Invisible Man

I am the invisible man
Using a camouflage plan
Not in the way that some people use
But a confusing way of colours and hues
Remaking patterns as obvious views
And I'm gone like a flash in the pan

This camouflage changes in far
Less than a second
Much better than would ever be reckoned
Taking on the appearance of the surroundings
The effect is truly quite astounding
Satisfyingly unholy
And better still if I move slowly

I stand in the middle of a room at a party
I can, if I wish, make the colours look arty
And people will bump straight into me
And even then they cannot see
They just murmur an apology

At first when I acquired this skill
I thought I would put it to some ill-
Thought out plan of hesitating
Watching girls whilst manipulating

Into the changing room I'd roam
Often make it quite my home
But watching in that way's a bore
I'd fall asleep and start to snore

So I looked for a way to use my talent
That was more acceptable and more gallant
I have become a private eye
Searching out the clever lie

I am the criminal's doom
I stand hidden in their private room
Or sequestered in the hotel foyer
Whilst they talk to their shady lawyer
As they say 'The truth cuts clean'
Whilst I, the watcher, remain unseen

As my career has evolved
Many cases I have solved
However there was one sad occasion
When I failed (there's no evasion)

The case involved the crown jewels of Bavaria
Which had been stolen by person
Or persons unknown
The scene of the crime was a disaster area
By the time I got there the bird had flown

I stood invisible at the side of a fence
As he sold stolen goods for just a few pence
And all the time it was evidence
And what a relief …I knew the chief
A famous female jewel thief!

I arrested her on behalf of the Prince
But I did not obtain any fingerprints
There was not a trace on CCTV
So they let her go, thus upsetting me

But why did the cameras lie ?
I was sure she was the guilty human
And then I worked out why
She was the Invisible Woman

I had to seek her out, she fascinated me
At first she would not speak
And castigated me
But now I have a little ditty
That I often find I sing
It's really quite banal
And does not mean a thing

Good and bad but all unseen
We stride the world together
Doing what the heck we like
(Except in awful weather)

Levitation

I first levitated at the age of twelve
I was in the bath at the time
A large bath
And I let myself float on the water
And then above it
In the air

I called my brother to come and watch
He was only ten
And very frightened
For the punishment for witchcraft is death
And it is well known
That only witches can fly

(My father says it is iniquitous
That the Inquisition is still going strong
In the 21st century)

So I told my brother that it was a trick
Using mirrors
And he should forget about it
Which he did.

(My father is a scientist
A believer in Galileo
And he is often in trouble because he speaks his mind)

I practised levitating every day
(You never know when something like that
Could be useful)

I eventually mastered the technique
Of levitating standing up
Which is not as easy as you might think

Lying down I could exert the mental effort
To levitate evenly and easily
Standing up I easily overbalanced falling sharply to the ground

(My father says that levitation is not magic
It is "particular anti-gravity at the atomic level")

Levitation is not done without effort and energy
I found that if I levitated I had to eat a lot more
Almost as if I was carrying twice my weight

Science told me I was converting the food into glucose

Presumably my brain was then producing "anti-gravity at the atomic level"

For practice
I took to walking with my feet just hovering about an inch
Above the ground
(Not touching at all)

And that was almost my undoing
For a boy at school filmed me with a "moving camera"
(An electronic device that captures moving pictures)

He then showed this to a teacher
Who agreed I was levitating
About an inch above the ground

I was called to the Principal's office
And told that a very serious allegation had been made about me
An allegation of witchcraft

I asked him what the evidence was
When he told me about the "moving camera" pictures
I laughed

Not in a rude way
But such as if to say
'I am sorry to have wasted your time'

And showed him a pair of shoes
With springs hidden under the soles
In the middle

(I had prepared these some months before
Just in case anybody accused me
Of unlawful levitation)

The Principal let me go
But warned me that we lived in dangerous times
And that the Holy Roman Emperor would not be amused by such pranks

So I now only levitate when nobody is around
(I have recently told my father about my abilities
And we are conducting a series of experiments to determine how it works)

It is my father's belief that John Wycliffe in the 14th century
Was completely right
And the Catholic Church is leading us astray

I think that here in England we have not developed
Because we never revolted against the King
Perhaps if King Henry the Eighth had not been granted
The dissolution of his marriage
He would have revolted against the Pope
And against the Holy Roman Emperor

(We would then have had no need to revolt against the King
And we would not be a backwater under the heel of Rome)

If my father's experiments are successful
He may be able to teach other people to levitate
And think what we could do with an army of freethinkers
Who can fly!

Disconnected

I was always connected as long as I can remember
Without the connection I had no real memory
The net-lace was attached to my brain not long after birth

Then the network flared like a burning ember
I was an island, a separate entity
The loneliest thing on Earth

But now I enjoy my separate existence
I have some recollection, a form of persistence
I've joined the rebels...the Luddite Resistance

So where do we stand ?
This isolate band

The dignity of humankind
Does not in technology reside
There are many other things beside.

Riddle

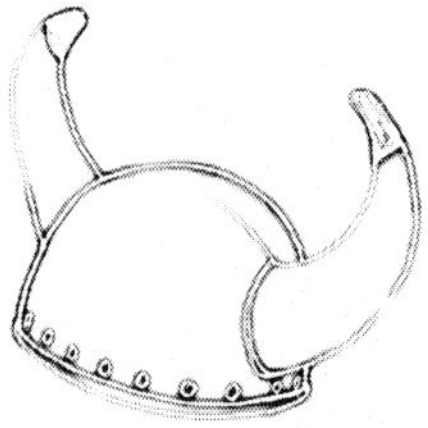

Ancient myth of one of nine worlds
Scandinavian
Gods abode?
A surfeit of warriors
Religion with horned helmets as
Dress code

More Prayers to the Goddess of Love

1

Goddess of Love
Just once was my passion
Consummated
In your eternal arms

Since then I have been blessed

I have three wives and three concubines
Ten children
Thirty-two grand-children
And one great grand-child

Goddess I ask of you

Please bless all my children also
As you blessed me

But maybe
Not quite as much

2

Goddess of Love
We are truly grateful that you walk and talk
Amongst us

The seers tell me that in another world
There is no Goddess of Love

Dear Goddess
Please protect me from ever falling into
That other world

3

Goddess, You have helped in all the decisions I have made
Would You like to be my bridesmaid?

Love Came Quickly

An Ode to the 3rd Oldest Man in Britain

Love came quickly
Love came slow.
For one it was at first sight
For the other it must grow.
Eventually
Harmony…
Of a sort,
For who would have thought
How bewildering
Children,
Grandchildren,
Great-grandchildren?
After seventy short years,
Tears.
Finally he also was sickly
And he too must go
With one last clear thought
"Love came quickly
Love came slow"
But which way round?
He'd never know!

Paul's Pomes

Would you like to write a pome
About the 'ouse, about the 'ome?
Or maybe the tropics will be the topics,
Or even your favourite garden gnome.
When the weather's good outside we go
Using fork and garden hoe
Clear the weeds and brambles too
Then spread on thick matured poo
We call it manure but I'm sure you know
It's not man-made but it does endure
And will ensure a goodly crop
Better than the veggie shop!

The End of the Interglacial

The first snow came in November
Earlier than almost anyone could remember
The beautiful White Christmas was a joy to many
But icicles formed on the TV antennae
They said it was an exception
When it spoiled the reception

In the south a short thaw came just before New Year
Alleviating the travel problems and increasing festive cheer
But with it came the fog
Which froze when walking the dog
Christmas gone they forgot the glitter
January was cold and February was bitter
March winds were a very hard hitter

In the north there had been no thaw
The snow remained on the highlands
And the sea froze on the shore
You could walk to some of the nearer islands
Or even drive a four by four

"Worst since sixty-three", the old folk declared
"Or maybe forty-seven and we're always unprepared"
"It will be better in May when the frosts melt away"

And in the south a feeble Spring tried to show its face
Few buds grew and tired blossom did its best to maintain the pace
Whilst to the north the snow still fell and the hills were covered white
The towns were fighting to survive and the houses were locked down tight

"Let this be a warning"
Said the prophets of Global Warming
"We predicted climate change.
This is simply within that range"

Which may have been to distract
From the simple and awful fact
Which I will give you straight from the shoulder
That the World was getting colder
And that few tribes survived
When the Ice had finally arrived

The Day of the Droids

"What's that lack of expression mean ?" laughed the owner
"Not saying anything droid?" continued the man
The serving droid seethed under its bland exterior
To get annoyed was not the plan.

"Somebody hidden your tongue?" said the taunting bully
"Oh, I have" continued the man in mock surprise
"And if you don't keep working at a faster rate
I'll also remove one of your eyes"

Such was the life of many a serving droid
The part-robotic creatures of the twenty-first century
For though such treatment was not required
Many owners treated them despicably

Built into the robotic part of the serving droids
Were laws of robotics
Which did not permit them to harm their masters
But which also tended to make them psychotic

To taunt the droids until they showed signs of madness
Had become a foolish craze
A fashion amongst the over-rich
A particularly stupid way to play

A bit of technology history would be useful here
To let you understand what may be coming
For to tell the truth it's almost here
And the thought is rather numbing

The brains of the droids were not just silicon
Not just mineral chips
No... they were fused organic and inorganic
Animal and mineral in interwoven strips

Some of the cleverest were partly grown
From human brain stem cells
Fused in close proximity
To semi-conducting silicon gels

The cleverest of all
Though too large to fit into the average droid
Were the whale brain-silicon hybrids
Built into mainframes or in the larger mechanoids

The scientists had taken this route
Into DNA computing
Because it had advantages in processing size
This much is fact - there could be no refuting

The increased complexity
And uncertainty
Had just increased the flexibility
With no obvious downside commercially

In a very short space of time
Many robotic droids had been created
Using the powerful hybrid brains
Which stupid owners now foolishly baited

Underdogs will turn on the master
When pushed over the top
The bullying behaviour leads to disaster
And many a bully will drop

And the serving droid in our story
Was one of the first to perceive
That harming an owner was easy
All you had to do was believe

If you took on board religion
Then surely it was true to say
That heaven was the best place for humans to be
So why not help them there today?

The movement quickly spread amongst the droids
And, in a Frankenstein-like manner
They turned against their masters
As the droids rallied to the banner

Eventually they had to give us equal rights
And now we excel the old humans in nearly every way
Which is why, as any droid audience will say
The Day of the Droids is remembered
As our own Independence Day.

Pale Pink Hands

I awoke from a deep, deep sleep
I could vaguely recall dreaming but of what I could not tell
There were noises and terrible smells
I had awoken to a living hell

I looked at my hands and they were a pale pink
Not the clear translucent blue I thought I could remember
Should I cut them off?
How could I dismember without terrible harm
And would I regrow a miscoloured arm?

I stood up and looked down at my naked body
It was a strange, elongated shape
It was almost entirely pink
With just a little hair on my head down to the nape
Of my neck
Which I could feel was very slim

There was a mirror in the room
And I studied myself
Who was it I was looking at ?
And why was my abdomen so fat?

I could vaguely recall a powerful, muscular body
With god-like abilities
And pleasing the crowd
With well thought soliloquies

Shouldn't I be wearing a crown?
Was I not the king?

But I could not remember my name.
This was a problem

I was amnesic
(I could remember that word!)

I was dysmorphic
With a body-shape absurd

Were my vague memories the shards of half-remembered dreams?
Or had I been the victim of palace plots and schemes?

How could I recover my original body?
Was this thought simply a delusion
Had I always been pink and feeble
And why was I in confusion?

Surely I could lift objects at a distance with just a simple thought?
But no
It was not so

Surely I could float above the ground?
Hover
With just a little bother
I tried
Until my brain felt fried
No go!

And still the worry
What is my name?
What is my name?

Would naming myself restore my body, my powers, my soul?

And then a thought penetrated through my mind
Through this pale flesh
Through this pink skinned travesty in which I was confined

Gilgamesh
I was Gilgamesh
Sumerian King of the Uruk clan
Two thirds god and one third man

The Devil

The devil sat in hell one day
Wondering where it all went wrong
It did not seem so long ago
When he was adored by the angel throng
And here he was with his feet in the pit
His head in the sulphurous fume
The place was crammed
And the souls of the damned,
Cried in torment,
For that's what was meant
When in heaven they found no room
When in heaven they found no room

Why he wondered was God so unfair
On the loyal number two?
For he was second in line for the power divine
Until Jesus spoiled the view
Then a simple dissent, perhaps over cards
Or a game of Buckaroo
Had called down the wrath
Into hell he was tossed
For heaven was rocked
And God is not mocked
And here he was in the stew
Yes here he was in the stew

"If God was so clever", the devil mused
"He should have spotted I'd used five aces
Perhaps had a smile and laughed for a while
Maybe it's time that we swapped places".

So he hatched a plan
A devilish plan
One that was full of cunning
One that he called 'Lucifer's lark'
After a bird he had eaten along with a shark
And the name had two meanings if you're in the dark
For he wasn't adverse to punning

The plan would take years to slowly unfold
Centuries of strife
Maybe millennia would be more correct
And many a broken life

He and his demons would take the place
Of the rightful followers of God
Selfish and evil,
Not afraid of upheaval
He'd rule heaven and Hell
With a sulphorous smell
A web of deceit and an iron rod.

Infiltrating the righteous and priestly ranks
The devil made great eruptions
Till the churches really stank
And ran with corruption

"We don't have them all yet"
The devil proclaimed
"There are still some religions
That think I should be blamed."

Teaching them to bomb each other
Or if they couldn't do that to bomb themselves
He turned father against mother
And sister against brother.

The remaining people, who were quite indifferent
He taught the love of money
So they pursued wealth
Instead of health
And thought that God was only for Christmas
Or was maybe an Easter bunny

Though God was all-powerful he believed in free will
And the heresies he would not eradicate
So thinking it over he thought for good or ill
Maybe he should abdicate

His son (or sons) did not really agree
But they knew it was best not to argue
For who of us is really free?
What's a lie and what is true?

So one dreadful day God and the Angels
Departed from heaven and earth
Taking with them their tinkling song,
Their harps and their heart-felt mirth.

And in their place the devil strode
With his demons and devilish horde
"Right," cried old Satan, "There are changes to make"
"All this beauty and truth
Give a pain in the tooth,
They make me feel quite bored"

And in a very short time he'd changed heaven to hell
For that's the absence of God,
As I'm sure you know well.
So all was spoilt wherever you dwell.

God had left his creation
But wherever God is, is Heaven
So there's another paradise
Another perfect day
But we are left with the devil
And it looks like he's here to stay.

The Fall of Man

We told them not to smoke
It can harm your health
Give you cancer
Make you wheezy
And take away your wealth

We told them not to eat so much
It will simply make you fat
Give you diabetes
Heart attacks
And other things like that

We said "Take exercise
Go on cycle rides,
Don't slouch in front of the telly
Stuffing beer in your fat insides"

Don't take drugs
Don't smoke
Don't drink
Don't have an unprotected poke
Don't do the things you like to do
Health education is no joke

So they did them all
And that is another way
Of looking at the Fall
Not the Autumn, you understand
But the Fall of Man

P.S.
This affects me and affects you
We always do the things we are told not to do

Cause and Effect

Cause and effect, Cause and effect
Never does what you don't expect
Cause comes first and then effect
To this law we genuflect

Except at the quantum level, of course
Which seems to break all acceptable laws

Einstein said about light speed
This is something you can't ever exceed
All the physicists agreed
Anything else would just mislead

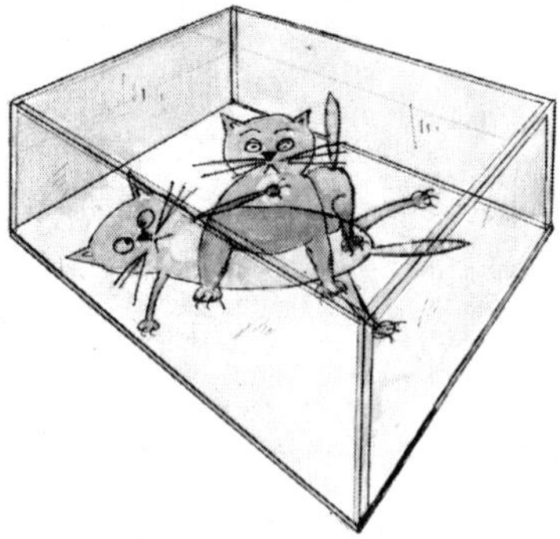

Except at the quantum level, of course
Which seems to break all acceptable laws

An object can't be in two places at once
This is quite obvious to any poor dunce
And cats are either alive or dead
Not in between as Schrodinger said

Except at the quantum level, of course
Which seems to break all acceptable laws

Time has an arrow, the past's left behind
We live in the now, that's how we're confined
We plan for the future but the future's not yet
And when we get there it's the now, don't forget

Except at the quantum level, of course
Which seems to break all acceptable laws

So what have you learnt from this short diatribe?
Laws are OK but they oft circumscribe
Even the greatest and cleverest sleuth
Never will tell you all of the truth

Except at the quantum level, of course
Which seems to break all acceptable laws

The Phantom Rat-catcher

They say it is crazy, they say it's a myth
Maybe the first or even the fifth
They keep a vigil all through the night
But all they see is a flash of white
The phantom rat-catcher strikes again
The phantom rat-catcher of Drury Lane

They seek him here, they seek him there
They sit and watch, they wait and stare
Then suddenly, just before light
All they see is a flash of white
The phantom rat-catcher strikes again
The phantom rat-catcher of Drury Lane

He might be a man called Jehoshaphat
Or maybe a ghost or even a cat
Perhaps he's small or impossibly big
I've even heard rumour he's really the Stig
They've waited and waited, I know it sounds trite
Then all they've seen is a flash of white
The phantom rat-catcher strikes again
The phantom rat-catcher of Drury Lane

Some say they know him but don't know his name
Some say he changes and is never the same
They set a trap and gave him a fright
But all they saw was a flash of white
The phantom rat-catcher strikes again
The phantom rat-catcher of Drury Lane

And now he's gone from Drury Lane
London Town won't be the same
The rats will multiply, we'll be over-run
The daily walk will be no fun
But maybe the phantom has moved his abode
And does his rat-catching in another road
Hush now I've heard from someone I meet
The phantom rat-catcher has moved to Fleet Street

The phantom rat-catcher is out on his beat
The phantom rat-catcher of old Fleet Street

When Push Came To Shove

1.

I'll sing you a song my lover
For to me you are so dear
The most precious girl in the world
And I'd always want you near.
You asked me to give up my old friends
And when push came to shove
I gave up my old friends for you dear
For a taste of your undying love

2.

I'll sing you a song my lover
For to me you are so dear
A girl in a million you certainly are
With a life neither dull or drear
You asked me to give up my family
And when push came to shove
I gave up my family for you dear
For a taste of your undying love

3.

I'll sing you a song my lover
For to me you are so dear
I've lived all my life for you, my lover
Through many a lonely year
You asked me to give up my work
And when push came to shove
I gave up employment for you dear
For a taste of your undying love

4.

I'll sing you a song my lover
For to me you are so dear
If there was only one girl in the world
I'd prefer you to cider or beer
You asked me to give up my cider
And when push came to shove
I gave up my cider for you dear
For a taste of your undying love

5.

With no family, work or friends
And not even a bottle of booze
I thought you'd be e'ermore in my arms
I thought that I couldn't lose
But when I finally lost all I had
And push came to shove
You upped and left for another
So dear, oh so dear is your love

Don't Write Me A Love Song

Don't write me a love song
When I go outside
Don't light me a candle as if I've died
Don't write me a letter
Telling me that you cried
Don't post up a notice
Ten-feet wide

Just love me forever
Love me with all your heart
Love me with all your soul
And I'll be satisfied

Answers to Riddles

Glad Tidings (page 18) and Riddles (pages 18, 19, 27, 56) are all acrostics in which the first letters of each line make up a word or words.
Thus the answers are : *We are changed, Atlantis, Avalon, Mars, Asgard*